THE COMPLETE ENGRAVINGS
OF MARTIN SCHONGAUER

THE
COMPLETE ENGRAVINGS OF
MARTIN SCHONGAUER

Edited and introduced by Alan Shestack

CURATOR OF DRAWINGS AND PRINTS, YALE UNIVERSITY ART GALLERY

Dover Publications, Inc., New York

Published in Canada by General Publishing Company, Ltd.,
30 Lesmill Road, Don Mills, Toronto, Ontario.

Published in the United Kingdom by Constable and Company, Ltd.,
10 Orange Street, London W.C.2.

The Complete Engravings of Martin Schongauer is a new work, first published by Dover Publications, Inc., in 1969. It consists of an Introduction by Alan Shestack, a list of illustrations and reproductions of all known engravings by Martin Schongauer, in chronological order in so far as possible.

Illustrations 3, 11, 13, 16, 22, 29, 34, 35, 38, 39, 44, 64, 65, 67, 98, 99, 102 and 103 are reproduced by courtesy of The National Gallery of Art, Rosenwald Collection.

Illustrations 7, 10, 26, 27, 28, 30, 31 and 33 are reproduced by courtesy of The National Gallery of Art, Gift of W. G. Russell Allen.

Illustration 12 is reproduced by courtesy of The Art Institute of Chicago.

Illustrations 110 and 113 were reproduced from Max Lehrs's *Geschichte und Kritischer Katalog des deutschen ... Kupferstichs im XV. Jahrhundert* (portfolio to Volume V, 1925), Gesellschaft für vervielfältigende Kunst, Vienna.

All other illustrations were reproduced from the portfolio *Martin Schongauer: Nachbildungen seiner Kupferstiche* (edited by Lehrs), Bruno Cassirer, Berlin, 1914.

Library of Congress Catalog Card Number: 68-29580

Manufactured in the United States of America

Dover Publications, Inc.
180 Varick Street
New York, N.Y. 10014

Introduction

Engraving was born in Germany just prior to the middle years of the fifteenth century. The new art form grew out of the discovery by goldsmiths that ink could be rubbed into designs incised on metal surfaces and then impressed upon paper. The potential of this printing process was quickly understood, and many craftsmen turned to the engraving of metal plates as an inexpensive method of multiplying their designs. Few of these early artisans signed their plates and their works are known to us today only as the products of anonymous hands. A few engravers initialed their works, however, and—in the tradition of medieval craftsmen—added their family hallmarks. These artists, such as Master E. S. and Master F. V. B., are identified by modern scholars according to the monograms which appear on their prints.

Unlike his anonymous predecessors, of whom no biographical traces remain, much of Martin Schongauer's life is documented. Schongauer, a painter as well as a printmaker, was by far the most accomplished engraver of the fifteenth century as well as the first in the history of German art whose name is known. In the archives and city library of Colmar, a town in the Upper Rhine valley south of Strasbourg, there is ample evidence that Schongauer lived, worked, and prospered there in the 1470's and 1480's. Schongauer's most famous painting, *The Madonna in the Rose Arbor*, which can still be seen in the church of St. Martin in Colmar, appears to have been completed by 1473. In 1488, Schongauer was summoned to Breisach, a town on the east bank of the Rhine some twenty miles from Colmar, to undertake the decoration of the interior walls of the cathedral with an enormous fresco of the Last Judgment. Schongauer died in Breisach in 1491, probably a victim of the plague which swept through the Upper Rhine area in that year. At some later time, his monumental paintings were irreverently covered with plaster, to be rediscovered only in 1931. They are visible today in the Breisach Münster, but in ruinous condition.

Although he was primarily a painter,[1] Schongauer also produced a corpus of one hundred sixteen engravings. Unlike painted panels and altarpieces, prints are easily transported. In the fifteenth century they were frequently sold at fairs and religious festivals. They were also acquired by artists and artisans and used in their workshops as sources of motifs and models for compositions. The exquisite style and impeccable craftsmanship of Schongauer's prints pleased his contemporaries no less than they charm us today, and his work became widely known and imitated throughout Europe.[2] We know that Schongauer's engravings appeared in Italy, where they were eagerly copied by Cristofano Robetta and Nicoletto da Modena. Vasari reports that *The Tribulations of St. Anthony* (Plate 4) so impressed and fascinated Michelangelo that he was inspired to paint a copy of it.[3] Schongauer's engravings also found their way to Nuremberg, where the young Albrecht Dürer saw and admired them. When Dürer finished his apprenticeship, he made his way to Colmar, hoping to meet Schongauer and, presumably, to work with him. Unfortunately, Dürer's route was a circuitous one and he arrived only after Schongauer had died in 1491. Dürer was welcomed by Schongauer's brothers, however, and was able to acquire from them several of Martin's early drawings. On one of these Dürer penned a note stating that the drawing was done by Martin in 1469; on another he indicated that the drawing was done in 1470 when Martin was an apprentice.[4] These statements in the handwriting of no less a personage than Albrecht Dürer provide fairly reliable evidence that Schongauer was an active artist by the end of the 1460's.

In many respects, Schongauer's prints represent a final flowering of the northern Gothic spirit. Their pious, devotional character and their emphasis on ornate drapery configurations ally them directly to the Gothic tradition. The courtly elegance of Schongauer's figures as well as their delicate facial types and gentle expressions also reveal Schongauer to be a late exponent of the so-called international Gothic style. This idyllic style, characterized by a sweetness of mood and by soft, flowing drapery patterns, flourished throughout Europe in the early years of the fifteenth century, but also had a lingering influence in the centers of art along the Rhine. Schongauer's mellifluous draftsmanship and tender conception of the human form relate him to the painters of the Burgundian court as well as to the school of Cologne, especially its leading master, Stephan Lochner.

At the same time that Schongauer represents Gothic draftsmanship at its ripest, however, his prints also exhibit the artist's sense for the essential, his inherent desire to simplify and organize. As he matured, Schongauer increasingly achieved an almost classical lucidity and decorum (see Plates 23, 100, 102).[5] In his later works, the individual figure or the single heraldic emblem silhouetted against a blank background becomes the dominant motif (Plates 40, 79–88, 93–96, 104, 105). Although the drapery breaks into complex, ornate folds, the folds are always carefully bunched and all the interior forms are contained within rigorous boundaries (Plates 23, 97). Moreover, the modeling of these crisp, angular folds is stringently controlled, with areas of shadow coalesced, forming sharp contrasts to the white planes. Schongauer uses dark and light not only to organize drapery, but also to mass and organize space and to enhance narrative clarity. In *Christ Before Annas* (Plate 26), for example, Christ's face stands out from the throng since it is an illuminated form placed against a densely hatched, dark background. The clothing of Annas, too, is scarcely modeled so that his figure clearly distinguishes itself from the richly modeled figures in the background. Thus, the confrontation of the two protagonists is clear, despite the fact that the stage is densely packed with forms. Similarly, in *The Entombment* (Plate 33) the figures of St. John and the Virgin on the near side of the sarcophagus are spotlighted against the group in shadow on the far side. The rock formation repeats and reinforces the basic vertical and horizontal lines of the composition.

The Schongauer family had its roots in the south German city of Augsburg. About 1440, Caspar Schongauer, a goldsmith, left his native city with his family and took up residence in Colmar. By 1445, Caspar was not only a citizen, but also a prominent member of the Colmar town council. Martin, one of Caspar's five sons, was probably born about 1450.[6] As he grew up, Martin must have spent many spare hours in his father's workshop where he became familiar with metalworking and where he mastered the handling of the goldsmith's burin. In his tiny engraving of two apprentices (Plate 58) Schongauer provides evidence of his familiarity with the goldsmith's shop. One of the scuffling youngsters wields a pair of tongs. To his right are a crucible and bellows, necessary equipment in a goldsmith's atelier. Several of Martin's prints also reveal his intimate knowledge of the kinds of artifacts produced by master goldsmiths (Plates 91, 92). In addition, Martin's ornament prints (Plates 108, 113–116) and leaf patterns (Plates 109–112) are in the tradition of goldsmiths' work and were probably intended for use as models by other goldsmiths and craftsmen. During the course of his career, Martin probably turned to engraving between his commissions for paintings. Ironically, most of his paintings have been destroyed or lost, while his entire graphic *œuvre* has survived and his fame today rests on the beauty and virtuosity of his engraved work.

The earliest document in which Martin Schongauer is mentioned is the matriculation book of the University of Leipzig. Martin's name appears along with the names of other students who began their studies in Leipzig in 1465.[7] He apparently found university studies incompatible with his artistic talents, for he did not register again in subsequent years.

FIG. 1.   *Roger van der Weyden,* The Nativity, *central panel of the* Bladelin Altarpiece *(courtesy of the Staatliche Museen Berlin, Gemäldegalerie Dahlem).*

It is generally assumed that Martin returned to Colmar, where, between 1466 and 1469, he was probably apprenticed to Caspar Isenmann, the municipal painter of Colmar and a neighbor of the Schongauer family. Isenmann's greatest work, the high altar of the Martinskirche, now in the museum in Colmar, was completed in 1465.[8] Like most Upper Rhenish painters of his time, Isenmann was greatly influenced by Flemish painting of the preceding generation, especially that of Roger van der Weyden, and he probably studied in the Netherlands. It was no doubt Isenmann who stimulated Schongauer's interest in Flemish painting and who may have encouraged him, upon the completion of his apprenticeship, to go to Burgundy to see the great altarpiece of the Last Judgment which Roger had painted for the hospital in Beaune. A Schongauer drawing of 1469, preserved in the Louvre,[9] is a direct and literal copy of the Christ from Roger's *Beaune Altarpiece*. When, some twenty years later in his career, Schongauer was himself confronted with the problem of creating a monumental image of the Last Judgment in the Breisach frescoes, he reverted to the Christ-type of Roger's painting.[10]

Schongauer's intimate knowledge of Roger's other paintings, as well as the echo in Schongauer's early work of the style of Dirk Bouts and Hugo van der Goes, suggests that Schongauer's travels took him down the Rhine to Cologne and then to the Netherlands. He probably got as far as Bruges and Middelburg in Zeeland, where he saw Roger's *Bladelin Altarpiece* (Figure 1), a painting which exercised great influence on Schongauer's early *Nativity* engraving (Plate 7). Schongauer's early work repeatedly betrays his profound debt to Netherlandish panel painting. His *Adoration of the Magi* (Plate 8) is a variation on Roger's *Columba Altarpiece*, which is now in Munich, but which was in Cologne in the 1460's. His *St. John the Baptist* engraving (Plate 13) is distinctly in the Netherlandish tradition and may be compared with the St. John in the Master of Flémalle's *Werl Altar*. The early *Madonna and Child with the Parrot* (Plate 6) is closely related to Dirk Bouts's Madonna in the National Gallery, London (Figure 2). Schongauer's thorough acquaintance with Flemish painting probably accounts for the composure, the impregnable dignity, and the sense of impeccable finish which characterize his engravings.

Some scholars feel that Schongauer, in addition to his trips to Burgundy and the Netherlands, also visited Spain during the formative years of his career. Several of his drawings, apparently portraits, are of so-called "Moorish" types. These types also populate the engravings as heathens, Roman soldiers, or Christ's tormentors. One art historian has also claimed

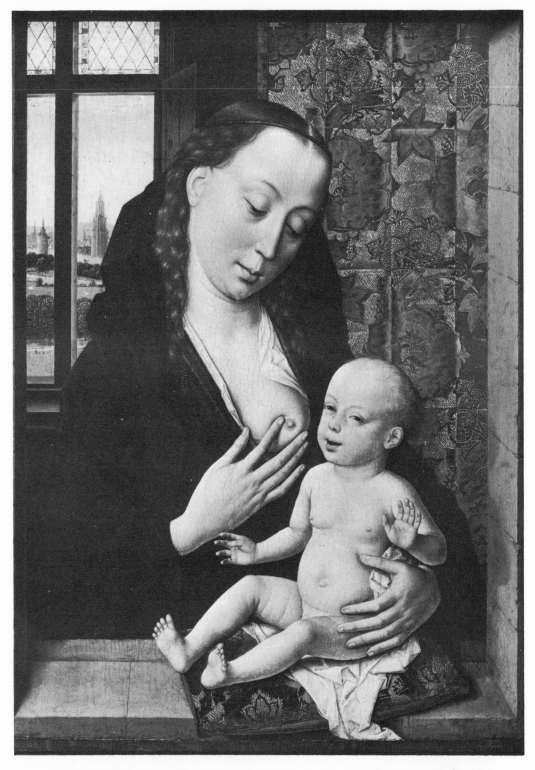

FIG. 2.   *Dirk Bouts,* Madonna and Child *(reproduced by courtesy of the Trustees, National Gallery, London).*

that the bust-length *Foolish Virgin* (Plate 103) bears an unmistakably Moorish appearance.[11] The hypothetical visit to Spain is given further support by the presence of a tropical date palm and dragon tree in *The Flight into Egypt* (Plate 9). Furthermore, one of Schongauer's major early works depicts St. James the Greater at the Battle of Clavijo. St. James is the patron saint of Spain and is venerated especially at Compostella in northwestern Spain, the goal of countless pilgrimages in the late middle ages. For many years, *The Battle of Clavijo* (Plate 11) was not accepted by many scholars as an authentic work by Schongauer. The eminent student of fifteenth-century engraving, Max Lehrs,[12] relegated the print to Schongauer's school. Recently, however, this engraving has been reconsidered and arguments for its authenticity have been put forward. The present writer has no doubt that it is an original Schongauer, but feels that it is an excessively ambitious and thus partially unsuccessful attempt by the youthful Schongauer to create a monumental battle scene.[13]

Although Schongauer monogrammed every print he created, he dated none of his plates. It had thus become a major task of scholarship to arrange his prints in a meaningful order, to establish a chronology through study of the evolution of the artist's style and technique. Although it would strain the capacity of stylistic analysis to place every print in exact relation to every other, it is possible to outline the main phases of Schongauer's development.[14]

A group of ten prints (Plates 1–10) stands out as Schongauer's earliest engraved work. Each of the ten is signed with a monogram which differs slightly from the monogram on all the later works: the two outer lines of the M are vertical parallels. In the later prints, these lines are diagonal, giving the M a more triangular shape. Characteristic of the ten early engravings is the vigorous but uncoordinated quality of the hatching. This is seen clearly in *The Man of Sorrows* (Plate 2), where undisciplined, comma-like strokes are employed on the flesh parts as well as on the drapery. Similar random modeling appears conspicuously on the hill behind the man and in the shadow cast by the horse in *The Peasant Family* (Plate 1). It is also found on the cloak of *St. Anthony* (Plate 4) and in the drapery of the Madonna in *The Nativity* (Plate 7).

The ten early prints must have been created just after 1470, when Schongauer returned to Colmar from his extensive travels. With the beauty of Flemish painting still fresh in his mind, it is no wonder that Schongauer's early prints betray an indebtedness to the style of Roger van der Weyden and Dirk Bouts. A few examples, in addition to those already cited, will suffice to point out the Flemish characteristics in Schongauer's early works. The Rogerian facial type of *The Madonna on the Crescent Moon* (Plate 3) is obvious, and the three figures in *The Man of Sorrows* (Plate 2) are closely related to the types in Roger's altarpiece of Jean de Bracque in the Louvre. We have already noted the compositional connection between *The Nativity* (Plate 7) and Roger's *Bladelin Altarpiece*. The Madonna in *The Adoration of the Magi* (Plate 8)—an engraving which bears some resemblance to Hugo van der Goes's *Monforte Altar* as well as to Roger's *Columba Altarpiece*—has strikingly Boutsian facial features.

Schongauer's early compositions are often highly complex, even to the point of being cluttered. In *The Madonna on the Crescent Moon* (Plate 3) the space is filled with irregular forms—the spidery nimbus of the Madonna and the stiffly drawn ribbon clouds at the bottom—which distract our attention from the main figure and animate the surface of the sheet. *The Death of the Virgin* (Plate 10) is characterized by an ornate tangle of line, the figures becoming enmeshed in the linear calligraphy.

Closely allied in style to the ten earliest engravings are Schongauer's two largest plates, *The Battle of Clavijo* (Plate 11) and *The Bearing of the Cross* (Plate 12). The latter is the largest engraving to have been created up to Schongauer's time. In grandeur of conception it goes beyond the bounds of printmaking and emulates panel painting. It is likely, indeed, that the composition is based on a lost painting by Jan van Eyck or one of his followers, a picture known only through a sixteenth-century copy in the museum in Budapest.[15] In the print, a great procession moves across the craggy landscape from right to left. At the extreme left the two thieves, already stripped of their clothing, are being led to Calvary. The darkly shaded rocky outcropping at the middle of the sheet draws our attention to the center and, together with the strong vertical element of the crossbar of the crucifix, creates a momentary halt in the ponderous movement of figures across the stage. At the center of the composition, Christ has fallen to his knees, crushed under the weight of the enormous cross. He peers out at us pitifully, involving us directly in his suffering. His face is physically and psychologically isolated from the throng of hostile thugs and tormentors by its location deep in the angle of the cross. The cross, in effect, enframes Christ's face as if it were an independent devotional image. This magnificent engraving is the final and most grandiose example of Schongauer's early pictorial style.

After this point there is an increasing tendency to limit and minimize pictorial elements in order to achieve greater harmony and compositional simplicity. In the later works the figures become more exquisite. Schongauer's roots in the workshop of his father and in the tradition of northern draftsmanship are still made manifest in the careful shaping of his beautiful drapery patterns and in the liveliness of his individual burin strokes. In the mature prints, however, there is a new restraint and decorum, and the outlines, especially those which describe the human form, become more supple. When landscape backgrounds appear, they are extremely reticent and their forms are carefully spread out, subordinated to the figures (see *Christ Appearing to the Magdalene*, Plate 98, and *The Baptism of Christ*, Plate 97). Unlike the more vigorous works of the early period, the later engravings emanate a gentle poetry.

Schongauer's technical evolution parallels his stylistic development. The short, hooked burin strokes of the early period are gradually lengthened, straightened, and stringently organized into networks of hatching and cross-hatching. When necessary, the long systematic lines are interspersed with short curved lines which follow the major contours and model every swelling and pocket of drapery. Schongauer's graphic vocabulary provided him with a precise means for creating solid form and for producing images which are impeccably tidy and finished in appearance.

The change in Schongauer's style can be seen in a comparison of *The Nativity* (Plate 99) done in Schongauer's mature years with an earlier treatment of the same subject (Plate 7). The most striking feature of the earlier work is the elaboration of the environment in which the scene occurs: the Gothic vault and the ivy-covered wall with its massive blocks. Joseph is given the greatest compositional prominence, even though he is only a spectator and does nothing more than hold a lantern. In the later engraving, Joseph is moved into the background. We see him on the left, returning to the stable after having found a midwife. The figures of the Madonna and Child are moved closer to us so that they dominate the scene. The Child, almost irrelevant in the earlier work, is framed by a bed of straw which serves as a kind of radiant halo. The diagonal poles of the hut intersect just behind the Madonna's halo, calling attention to her face and repeating the diagonals of her crossed arms. Even the back of the donkey is a firm compositional line. The entire composition is extremely rational. And, just as the composition is more precise, so are the modeling lines more regular and schematically organized.

A telling comparison can also be made between the early *Tribulations of St. Anthony* (Plate 4) and the mature *St. Lawrence* (Plate 104). The St. Anthony print is highly animated. We are left with the impression of a conglomeration of sharp, spiky, irregular and tortuous forms. The *St. Lawrence* by comparison is the ultimate in formal economy. A simple columnar figure is isolated like a piece of statuary against a blank background. The contours of the saint's alb and tunic are straight and simple, spreading out slightly on the ground to form a sort of pedestal which firmly anchors the figure. The tectonic organization of form extends even to the face with its clear, regular features. In perfect harmony with the handsome, aristocratic figure is the articulate graphic language. The drapery folds are precisely defined by the contrasts of light and dark as well as through the use of strictly controlled cross-hatching in the deepest shadows.

The reticence of Schongauer's late style is also seen in the series of *The Wise and Foolish Virgins* (Plates 79–88) and in the four roundels of the evangelists' symbols (Plates 93–96). *The Angel of St. Matthew* (Plate 93) is composed with especial care. The figure is fitted perfectly into the round border and the angel's head is beautifully enframed by the pattern of his wings. To implant the figure on the ground and to give stability to the vertical axis, Schongauer exaggerated the distance between waist and knee. The crisp drapery folds stand in gentle counterpoint to the flowing contours of the empty banderole.

Perhaps the most perfect example of Schongauer's final style is found in his late *Annunciation* (Plates 106, 107). To be sure, the long, thin fingers, the elegant curly hair, the ornate drapery folds and the banderole which flutters around Gabriel's scepter are symptoms of a somewhat mannered Gothic attitude. All of the linear play, however, is subjected to stringent control. For one thing, the angel and Madonna appear on two separate plates. The division of the two splendid figures into two distinct images is in full accord with Schongauer's deliberate attempt in his late work to achieve absolute monumentality. The angel's only accessory is his scepter; the Madonna is accompanied only by an elegant lily which symbolizes her purity. The scene takes place in an abstract space rather than in the Virgin's chamber and the extremely corporeal figures are silhouetted against a bare background. The drapery in which their forms are swathed is fully modeled, giving each convexity convincing bulk and weight. These two prints thus represent Schongauer's final style, the late Gothic in Germany at its ripest, and also at its most lucid. Undoubtedly, Dürer was attracted to Schongauer's work because he sensed in it the unity and clarity of form which he was to find later only in Italy in the paintings of Mantegna and Bellini.

New Haven, Connecticut   ALAN SHESTACK
1968

Notes

1. The basic work on Schongauer's paintings is Ernst Buchner, *Martin Schongauer als Maler*, Berlin, 1941; see also Alfred Stange, *Deutsche Malerei der Gotik*, VII, Munich–Berlin, 1955, pp. 17–24.

2. Copies after Schongauer are enumerated by Alfred Schmid, "Copien nach Kupferstichen von Schongauer," *Repertorium für Kunstwissenschaft*, XV, 1892, pp. 19–25; W. Thöllden, *Die Wirkung der Schongauerstiche auf die deutsche Plastik um 1500*, Dresden, 1938. For the use of prints in sculptors' ateliers see Justus Bier, "Riemenschneider's Use of Graphic Sources," *Gazette des Beaux-Arts*, 6th series, L, 1957, pp. 203–222.

3. Giorgio Vasari, *Lives of the Most Eminent Painters, Sculptors, and Architects*, trans. by G. Duc. de Vere, VI, London, 1912–14, pp. 91–92.

4. The latter drawing is unfortunately lost. The former is preserved in the British Museum and reproduced in Jakob Rosenberg, *Martin Schongauer Handzeichnungen*, Munich, 1923, no. 37, and in Franz Winzinger, *Die Zeichnungen Martin Schongauers*, Berlin, 1962, no. 2, p. 30. Friedrich Winkler and other scholars have argued that the drawing is not an authentic Schongauer, but a Dürer copy of a Schongauer drawing of 1469. See F. Winkler, *Die Zeichnungen Albrecht Dürers*, I, Berlin, 1936, p. 15 ff.

5. Schongauer's classicism is brilliantly discussed by Ulrich Middeldorf, "Martin Schongauers klassischer Stil," *Deutsche Beiträge zur geistigen Überlieferung*, Chicago, 1947, pp. 94–114.

6. Schongauer's birth date used to be set as early as 1430. The authors of the two most recent monographs, however, propose a birth date about 1450. See Julius Baum, *Martin Schongauer*, Vienna, 1948, p. 8 and Eduard Flechsig, *Martin Schongauer*, Strasbourg, 1951, pp. 1–33. For a contrary view placing Schongauer's birth at about 1435 see A. Stange, *Deutsche Malerei*, VII, pp. 17–19.

7. This document and all other documentary evidence on the life of Schongauer is listed in Baum, *Schongauer*, pp. 66–71.

8. See Gisela Bergsträsser, *Caspar Isenmann, Ein Beitrag zur oberrheinischen Malerei des 15. Jahrhunderts*, Colmar, 1941, and A. Stange, *Deutsche Malerei*, VII, pp. 12–15, pls. 13–17. Documentation showing that Isenmann lived in the Schedelgasse, the same street in which the Schongauer house was located, is found in E. Waldner, "Urkundliches über Colmarer Maler des 15. Jahrhunderts," *Zeitschrift für die Geschichte des Oberrheins*, LIII, 1899, p. 69.

9. Reproduced in Rosenberg, *Schongauer Zeichnungen*, no. 23, and in Winzinger, *Die Zeichnungen Schongauers*, pl. 4.

10. Reproduced in Baum, *Schongauer*, pl. 211.

11. Flechsig, *Schongauer*, pp. 203–206.

12. Max Lehrs, *Geschichte und Kritischer Katalog des deutschen, niederländischen und französischen Kupferstichs im XV. Jahrhundert*, V, Vienna, 1925, p. 376.

13. My arguments are presented in Alan Shestack, *Fifteenth Century Engravings of Northern Europe from the National Gallery of Art*, Washington, 1967, no. 42; the aforementioned catalogue provides iconographical information and stylistic observations on eighty-one of Schongauer's prints.

14. The first attempt to place Schongauer's prints in chronological sequence was Hans Wendland, *Martin Schongauer als Kupferstecher*, Berlin, 1907; for a critique of Wendland's method see Max J. Friedländer, "Martin Schongauers Kupferstiche," *Zeitschrift für bildende Kunst*, N.F. XXVI, 1915, pp. 105–112; one of the best chronologies is that of Max Geisberg in the Schongauer entry of the Thieme-Becker *Künstlerlexikon*, XXX, 1936, pp. 249–254. In addition, Geisberg provides a thorough listing of the literature up to 1936. The footnotes in Baum, *Schongauer*, also provide an excellent bibliography.

15. See Robert A. Koch, "Martin Schongauer's 'Christ Bearing the Cross,'" *Record of the Art Museum, Princeton University*, XIV, 1955, pp. 22–30. Lilli Fischel has recently suggested that *The Tribulations of St. Anthony* (B.47) also has an Eyckian source. See "Zu Schongauers Heiligem Antonius," *Studien zur Kunst des Oberrheins, Festschrift für Werner Noack*, Konstanz-Freiburg, 1958, pp. 92–98.

List of Illustrations

The dimensions are given in millimeters (100 mm = 3.937 inches), height before width; for plates with engraved borders, it is the measurements of the borders that are given. The B numbers are those of the Bartsch catalogue, the L numbers those of the Lehrs catalogue.

1. Peasant Family Going to Market, 163 × 163, B.88, L.90.
2. The Man of Sorrows with the Virgin and St. John (first state), 225 × 165, B.69, L.34.
3. The Madonna on the Crescent Moon, 173 × 109, B.31, L.40.
4. The Tribulations of St. Anthony (second state), 312 × 230, B.47, L.54.
5. St. George and the Dragon, 85 mm diameter, B.51, L.58.
6. The Madonna and Child with the Parrot (first and second states), 158 × 109, B.29, L.37.
7. The Nativity, 258 × 170, B.4, L.5.
8. The Adoration of the Magi, 256 × 168, B.6, L.6.
9. The Flight into Egypt, 255 × 169, B.7, L.7.
10. The Death of the Virgin (first state), 255 × 169, B.33, L.16.
11. The Battle of St. James at Clavijo, 289 × 432, B.53, not accepted by Lehrs.
12. The Bearing of the Cross, 286 × 430, B.21, L.9.
13. St. John the Baptist, 154 × 114, B.54, L.59.
14. St. Agnes, 153 × 103, B.62, L.67.
15. St. Martin, 155 × 106, B.57, L.62.
16. The Madonna and Child with the Apple, 173 × 125, B.28, L.39.
17. The Crucifixion, 290 × 196, B.25, L.14.
18. The Crucifixion, 106 × 72, B.22, L.10.
19. The Crucifixion, 117 × 84, B.23, L.12.
20. The Crucifixion (first and second states), 107 × 73, unknown to Bartsch, L.11.
21. The Madonna and Child on a Grassy Bench, 122 × 84, B.30, L.36.
22. St. John on Patmos, 160 × 114, B.55, L.60.
23. The Madonna and Child in the Courtyard, 166 × 119, B.32, L.38.

24–35 PASSION SERIES

24. Christ on the Mount of Olives, 164 × 116, B.9, L.19.
25. The Betrayal of Christ, 164 × 116, B.10, L.20.
26. Christ Before Annas, 163 × 114, B.11, L.21.
27. The Flagellation, 163 × 116, B.12, L.22.
28. Christ Crowned with Thorns, 161 × 113, B.13, L.23.
29. Christ Before Pilate, 162 × 115, B.14, L.24.
30. Ecce Homo, 161 × 112, B.15, L.25.
31. The Bearing of the Cross, 163 × 115, B.16, L.26.
32. The Crucifixion, 162 × 115, B.17, L.27.
33. The Entombment, 163 × 116, B.18, L.28.
34. Christ in Limbo, 166 × 115, B.19, L.29.
35. The Resurrection, 163 × 116, B.20, L.30.

36. The Crucifixion, 195 × 150, B.24, L.13.
37. The Annunciation, 162 × 112, B.3, L.1.
38. St. Michael, 162 × 113, B.58, L.63.
39. St. Christopher, 160 × 112, B.48, L.56.
40. The Madonna and Child, 88 × 61, B.27, L.35.
41. Christ in an Attitude of Benediction, 85 × 59, B.68, L.32.
42. The Christ Child in an Attitude of Benediction, 88 × 61, B.67, L.31.
43. St. Anthony, 88 × 62, B.46, L.53.
44. A Bishop, 89 × 61, B.61, L.55.

45–56 THE SERIES OF APOSTLES

45. St. Peter, 89 × 43, B.34, L.41.
46. St. Andrew, 89 × 44, B.35, L.43.
47. St. James the Great, 89 × 43, B.36, L.44.
48. St. John, 90 × 50, B.37, L.45.
49. St. Philip, 89 × 50, B.38, L.48.
50. St. Bartholomew, 90 × 50, B.39, L.49.
51. St. Judas Thaddaeus, 89 × 44, B.40, L.52.
52. St. Matthias, 89 × 50, B.41, L.50.
53. St. James the Less, 88 × 43, B.42, L.47.
54. St. Simon, 90 × 51, B.43, L.51.
55. St. Thomas, 90 × 50, B.44, L.46.
56. St. Paul, 90 × 44, B.45, L.42.

57. St. George and the Dragon, 58 × 74, B.50, L.57.
58. Apprentices Fighting, 57 × 74, B.91, L.87.
59. Two Moors in Conversation, 90 × 50, B.90, L.89.
60. A Miller with Two Donkeys, 87 × 124, B.89, L.88.

Illustrations

1. *Peasant Family Going to Market*

2. The Man of Sorrows with the Virgin and St. John

3. The Madonna on the Crescent Moon

4. *The Tribulations of St. Anthony*

5. St. George and the Dragon

6. *The Madonna and Child with the Parrot (first state)*

6. *The Madonna and Child with the Parrot (second state)*

7. *The Nativity*

8. *The Adoration of the Magi*

9. The Flight into Egypt

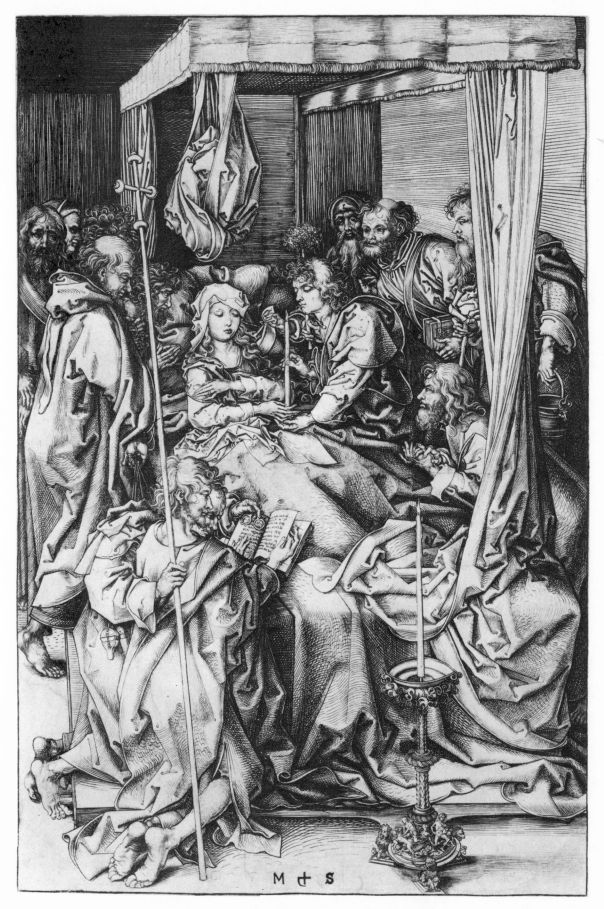

10. *The Death of the Virgin*

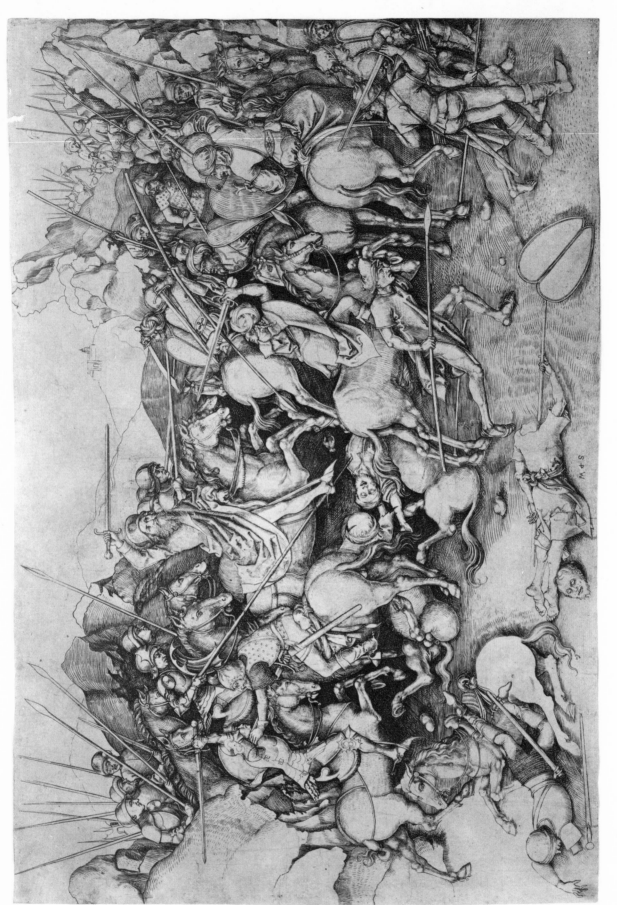

11. *The Battle of St. James at Clavijo*

12. *The Bearing of the Cross*

13. St. John the Baptist

14. *St. Agnes*

15. *St. Martin*

16. *The Madonna and Child with the Apple*

17. *Crucifixion*

21. *The Madonna and Child on a Grassy Bench*

Nos. 18–20 are on the following double-page spread.

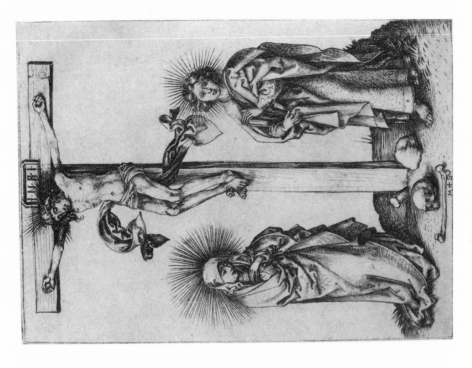

19. *Crucifixion*

18. *Crucifixion*

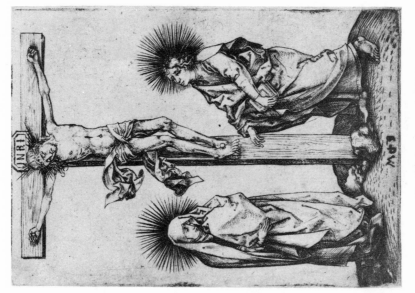

20. *Crucifixion (first state)*

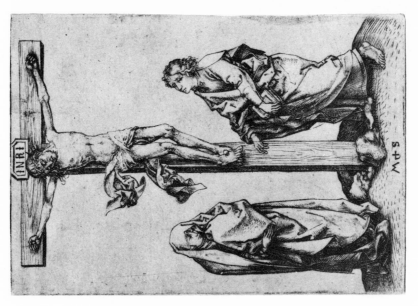

20. *Crucifixion (second state)*

22. St. John on Patmos

23. *The Madonna and Child in the Courtyard*

24. The Passion: Christ on the Mount of Olives

25. The Passion: The Betrayal of Christ

26. The Passion: Christ Before Annas

27. The Passion: The Flagellation

28. The Passion: Christ Crowned with Thorns

29. *The Passion: Christ Before Pilate*

30. *The Passion: Ecce Homo*

31. *The Passion: The Bearing of the Cross*

32. The Passion: The Crucifixion

33. *The Passion: The Entombment*

34. *The Passion: Christ in Limbo*

35. The Passion: The Resurrection

36. The Crucifixion

37. The Annunciation

38. St. Michael

39. *St. Christopher*

40. *The Madonna and Child*

41. *Christ in an Attitude
of Benediction*

42. *The Christ Child in an Attitude
of Benediction*

43. *St. Anthony*   44. *A Bishop*

45. *The Apostles:*
St. Peter

46. *The Apostles:*
St. Andrew

47. *The Apostles:*
St. James the Great

48. *The Apostles:*
St. John

49. *The Apostles:*
St. Philip

50. *The Apostles:*
St. Bartholomew

51. *The Apostles:*
St. Judas Thaddaeus

52. *The Apostles:*
St. Matthias

53. *The Apostles:*
St. James the Less

54. *The Apostles:*
St. Simon

55. *The Apostles:*
St. Thomas

56. *The Apostles:*
St. Paul

57. St. George and the Dragon

58. Apprentices Fighting

59. *Two Moors in Conversation*

60. *A Miller with Two Donkeys*

61. *A Family of Pigs*

62. *Stag and Doe*

64. *St. Sebastian*

63. *St. Sebastian*   65. *St. Veronica*

66. *St. Catherine*   67. *St. Barbara*

68. St. Catherine

69. *Shield with a Lion, Held by an Angel*

70. *Shield with a Unicorn, Held by a Seated Lady*

71. *Shield with a Swan, Held by a Seated Lady*

72. *Shield with Three Stars, Held by a Standing Lady*

73. *Shield with a Lion's Head, Held by*
a Wild Woman

74. *Shield with a Griffin's Foot and Shield with a Rooster,*
Held by a Moor

75. *Shield with Wings, Held by*
a Seated Peasant

76. *Shield with a Greyhound, Held by*
a Wild Man

*77. Shield with a Stag, Held by
a Wild Man*

*78. Shield with a Hare and Shield with a Moor's Head,
Held by a Wild Man*

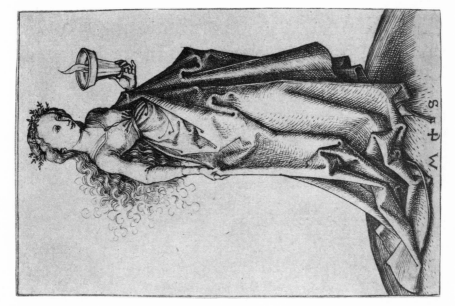

80. *A Wise Virgin*

79. *A Wise Virgin*

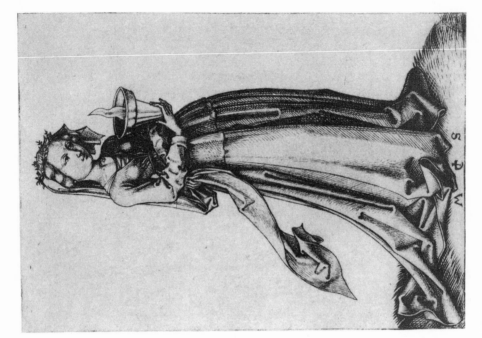

82. *A Wise Virgin*

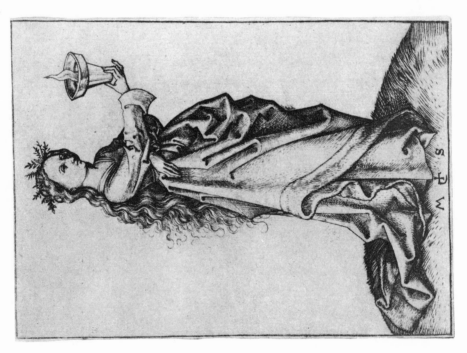

81. *A Wise Virgin*

83. *A Wise Virgin*

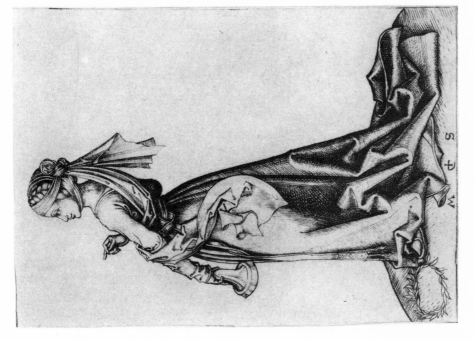

84. *A Foolish Virgin*

85. *A Foolish Virgin*

86. *A Foolish Virgin*

88. *A Foolish Virgin*

87. *A Foolish Virgin*

89. The Griffin

90. *The Elephant*

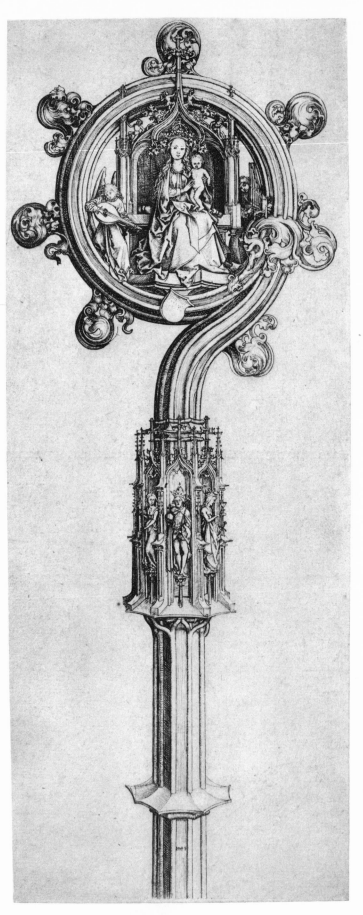

91. *A Bishop's Crozier*

92. *A Censer*

93. The Evangelists:
The Angel of St. Matthew

94. The Evangelists:
The Ox of St. Luke

95. *The Evangelists:*
The Lion of St. Mark

96. *The Evangelists:*
The Eagle of St. John

97. The Baptism of Christ

98. *Christ Appearing to the Magdalene*

99. *The Nativity*

100. *Christ Enthroned*

101. *The Coronation of the Virgin*

102. *Christ Blessing the Virgin*

104. *St. Lawrence*

No. 103 follows no. 107

105. *St. Stephen*

106. *The Annunciation: The Angel Gabriel*

107. *The Annunciation: The Virgin*

103. *A Foolish Virgin*

108. *Ornament with Owl Mocked by Day Birds*

110. *Thistle Ornament*

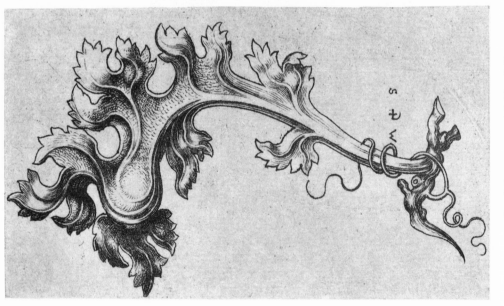

109. *Leaf Ornament with Tendril*

112. *Leaf Ornament*

111. *Leaf Ornament*

113. *Vine Ornament*

114. *Vine Ornament with Birds*

115. Ornament with Hop Vine

116. Leaf Ornament